REBUILDING YOUR LIFE

After Homicide

Victim Support Services

Rebuilding Your Life after a Homicide
is published by:
Families and Friends of Missing Persons and
Violent Crime Victims
dba Victim Support Services
P.O. Box 1949
Everett, WA 98206-1949
Phone: 425-252-6081
24-hour hotline 1-888-288-9221
Visit our Website: victimsupportservices.org

Fifth revised edition, May 2016

Fourth revised edition, July 2010

Third revised edition, May 2004

Second revised edition, Copyright August 1991

Copyright May 25, 1983

ISBN-13: 978-1533134059

All rights reserved. No part of this book may be reproduced in any form or by any mechanical means, including information retrieval systems without permission in writing from the publisher, except by a reviewer who may quote brief passages in a review of this work.

Additional copies of this book may be ordered

Dedication

To all those who have been hurt or harmed by homicide. You and your loved ones are in our hearts. May they never be forgotten.

Preface

Victim Support Services (VSS), formerly *Families and Friends of Missing Persons and Violent Crime Victims*, originally published this in 1983, and titled "Grief by Homicide", to provide family members and friends a resource and guide to turn to when a loved one is murdered. This book was written by survivors who had gone through a horrific tragedy and wanted to provide a resource compiling information that they wish they knew before their journey began. Today, this book has been updated to include the most relevant information and research to assist you in your journey.

The new title of this book, "Rebuilding your Life after Homicide" has been chosen because it reflects the experience that surviving victims of homicide undergo after the unthinkable happens. Survivors report that they literally had to pick up the pieces of the old, and find a new way to carry on. Rebuilding a new normal and a new way of living. Life as they knew it was different after the violent loss of their loved one.

The most important message of this book is to convey that you are not alone. Many mothers, fathers, husbands, wives, sisters, brothers, aunt's, uncle's, steps, grandparents, and close friends have walked a similar path before you. Losing a loved one to homicide is a very misunderstood form of grief, no one is prepared for such a sudden and violent act. We are sorry that you are going through this.

This book was written with you, your loved one, and your family in mind. Everyone's story is unique. There is no blue print available to get you through this. There is no right way to grieve or recover.

This book has been developed as a guide of what you might expect along the way. This journey will not be easy. It will take everything that you have to make it through it, there will be really difficult moments, as well as positive ones. You are not alone, agencies like Victim Support Services are across the United States to help guide you through this process. Please don't hesitate to reach out to someone if you need help. Turn to the resource chapter in the back of the book for an organization that might be able to assist you.

Victim Support Services depends on donations to continue the important work that they do providing support to family and friends of homicide victims. If you would like to help you can donate online at www.victimsupportservices.org or by sending check to PO Box 1949 Everett WA 98206.

Contents

Introduction 9

1. Initial Thoughts and Feelings 11
2. Coping 22
3. After the Murder 28
4. The Criminal Justice System 36
5. Civil Remedies 60
6. Crime Victim Rights 66

Other Reading 68

Resources 70

Glossary of Terms 72

Introduction

This book is for you, because someone you love has been the victim of homicide. It is impossible to conceive of homicide happening to someone close to you. Your anger, pain and grief will be extensive. It will take time, internal resolve, and support from family, friends, colleagues, counselors, and sometimes strangers or advocates to rebuild your life, and to create what will be a new normal. It will be a different life but you can go on.

This booklet, originally titled "Grief by Homicide" was prepared for you by others who have lived through the murder of someone they love. It is our way of reaching out with understanding and compassion as you travel your journey of reconstruction.

Rebuilding Your Life After Homicide

After you learn of the death of your loved one, your life is irrevocably changed. *Victim Support Services* has worked with thousands of victims who became survivors. Others have traveled the journey you are facing. What follows are their experiences and what they have learned along the way through their journey of grief to healing. It also contains information you may need at critical points on this difficult journey.

Take your time going through these chapters, some of this information you may have heard before, some of it you may be hearing for the first time. You may relate to some experiences or information and/or some of the information you may disagree with. That's okay. There is not a one size fits all experience after something like this happens. Everyone's experience and story is unique. Take what fits for you, and let go of what doesn't. Feel free to skip around in the book and write in the margins. This your guide book, use it as you see fit.

Chapter 1

Initial Thoughts and Feelings

There is a rush of emotions after the devastating news that a loved one has been murdered. Numbness, shock, and disbelief are typical reactions in those first difficult days. You may discover that you are more forgetful and your memory and thought processes are scattered. Some survivors have stated that they didn't even feel present in their bodies and they walked around in a fog, unable to emotionally or mentally connect to anything going on around them. Others have said life felt like a constant state of confusion and nothing made sense anymore.

There is never a right or wrong way to react to murder. You may have heard of people speak of the 'stages of grief'. There are no specific steps you go through in any particular order. Everyone deals with this kind of loss differently. However you are feeling, know you are not going crazy and you are not wrong for how you feel or react. There may be frequent moments when your mind tries to deny the crime even happened and you find yourself mentally trying to make 'deals' with the universe to bring back your loved one.

During these first days in the aftermath of a traumatic loss, remember to take care of yourself. Drink lots of water, get rest, and listen to your bodies' needs. These basic tasks will help you cope and function. Once the numbness and shock have worn off there will be other emotions that may feel just as overwhelming. Survivors sometimes report feelings of intense anger and guilt.

Anger

Understandably after such a horrific event survivors of homicide can be very angry. You may find yourself angry at the offender, the victim, other surviving family members, law enforcement, the criminal justice system, actually just about anyone. It is easy to lash out, looking for a way to lessen the overwhelming feeling of losing your loved one.

Know that your anger is coming from a place of hurt and unimaginable loss. Wanting to resolve those feelings of loss can make survivors want to place blame on someone right away and make them 'pay'. Sometimes this anger can be misdirected at those around you. While it is understandable to be angry at anyone near you, the perpetrator is responsible for the crime and your loss. The slow moving criminal justice process can often only add fuel to that anger. Talking to others who have experienced your kind of loss can help.

Your feelings of anger are a typical experience among survivors. You may end up using the energy behind that anger to help move you through the criminal justice process once an arrest is made.

Guilt

In many cases, there is a measure of guilt survivors may feel. Each survivor lives with the "what if's". "What if I had gone over to his house before he was murdered?" "Why didn't I ask her out for dinner?" "What if I had knocked the gun out of his/her hand?" These are very typical thoughts. Focusing on those 'what ifs' will keep you stuck in a sense of guilt and denial. Please remember that one cannot predict the future or what might have been. You can't change the events that took place. Berating yourself is destructive and will hinder the grieving process. Guilt is an emotion that tries to change events that cannot be changed.

The details surrounding the murder of your loved one may be difficult to hear but may provide evidence necessary to ease your own sense of guilt. All these fragments of information will form into the fabric of your story. With time, the unknowns will lessen, and the 'what ifs' will fade. Ultimately, it is important to remember that the fault of the murder lies solely in the hands of the perpetrator(s). Nothing you did or didn't do caused your loved one's death.

Revenge

It is a typical reaction to have feelings of revenge. Someone has violently taken your loved one from you. It makes sense that you would want that person to feel the same pain you do. You may feel as if you are stuck in this feeling, and that revenge is the only thing that can make you feel better. Understandably, some people are disturbed by this emotion. Most people we have worked with have expressed this feeling. Not one has ever acted upon it. There will be those who will tell you that wanting revenge is unhealthy and that the only way you can find peace is to forgive. If forgiveness is in your heart, then forgive, but do not allow others to place unnecessary guilt on you. Chances are they have never been where you are.

Your choice to forgive what seems to be the unforgivable is a very personal and private decision. There are no right or wrong choices with regard to this. Just know that feelings of hate, disgust, and desire for revenge against the perpetrator are all very normal as well. As you process the terrible events during the days ahead, your feelings will be clarified for you.

Spirituality

You may find that your spirituality or faith has been shaken. You may find that there has been a change in your view of the world. You may have difficulty trusting, believing everyone or everyday situations to be harmful or dangerous. Constant exposure to violence through the media or your own life can skew how you look at society and those around you. Surrounding yourself with good people and seeing the positive things in the world can help restore your balance. Some find that they are angry with God; they ask, "Why does a just God allow this horrible tragedy to happen?" or "If there is a God, he would have prevented this from happening." Many loved ones of homicide victims had strong faith before, yet subsequently find going to houses of worship too painful. Given time and support from the religious community, many have been able to rebuild their faith with a renewed and deeper understanding of the tenets of their religion.

Forgiveness is oftentimes centered around our faith. Whether forgiveness is something you have thought about or others have encouraged you to do, it will need to be a personal decision. We have had people say that after forgiving the person who committed the crime they were able to let go of those negative emotions. The forgiveness was chosen for themselves, for their own healing and peace of mind. Ultimately, forgiveness may or may not be part of your grief journey.

Relationship Dynamics

The grieving process

Each individual grieves in their own way. How we grieve is determined by many things, including our personal view of death, how society views death, and individual personalities.

Remember that people are different. There is no one way to handle violent death. What works for you may not work for others. It is also important to realize that men and women may grieve very differently. While every person is an individual, there are some common traits that are seen with the grieving styles of men and women. It is common for women to process their grief by talking through their feelings. They may need to verbalize and process their grief, talk about their lost loved one and relive memories from the past. Men are not generally focused on talking grief out in the same manner. Men may focus on "doing things" and "fixing things" which is difficult after a homicide. Death cannot be fixed and men may feel powerless, not knowing what to do. They may not want to re-hash the sadness of the event and they may not know how to respond to the emotions being expressed by the loved ones around them. This may make relationships difficult as women feel that their male loved ones are not grieving as deeply or being supportive as needed. Men may feel that talking about the event does not make it any better. Understanding that these differences exist may make it easier for families to acknowledge and respect different communication styles.

Many people expect that tragedy brings families closer together, and this may or may not be the case for you. Dynamics in families are often complicated and traumatic events, such as losing a loved one to homicide can often intensify these complicated dynamics. It is not unusual for us to see families separate, both physically and emotionally. In some cases, families are drawn closer together, often because they are able to communicate their needs, ask for help, and seek compassion and understanding.

Sometimes people don't know what to say to you, and may avoid you. This can be hurtful. Other times people will say or ask inappropriate questions. Often, people have good intentions but they just don't know how to best support you. It helps to share your feelings, and needs so that they know how to best support you.

Meeting new people can be difficult. And you might not want to engage with new people and have to share your story over and over. Sometimes seeking out people who have shared similar experiences, such as through a support group, can be helpful. Individuals who have lost loved ones to violent crimes may be able to understand what you are experiencing in a way that others cannot.

You may develop relationships with other support people outside your circle of friends and family, such as victims' advocates, or a counselor. It can often be very helpful to have someone to lean on who has experience with the dynamics of crime victimization who can give you tools to help you cope. You may find that relationships with

Victim Support Services

professionals such as a counselor or advocate are especially helpful.

More often than not your support system will look very different than before the homicide occurred. You may find yourself reconnecting with people you have previously lost touch with, and you may find previously close relationships become strained or distant. No matter who you lean on for support, having a strong support system can make coping after a homicide easier.

Holidays

Holidays are an accumulation of traditions. Traditions are habits made by families to be shared by its members. When a member of the family is no longer there to share the tradition that was once cherished, holidays can become a painful reminder instead of a joyful time.

The first time you celebrate each holiday after a death can be challenging. Old traditions may seem empty or painful without your loved one there to celebrate with you. Birthdays can be a reminder of another year that has gone by without your loved one.

You may want to develop new traditions. Some people choose to honor their loved one in a special way during celebrations. Some choose to take a step back from celebrating, or let others do the hard work. There is no rule to follow on how to "get through" a holiday. Give yourself permission to do whatever feels right to you.

Societal Expectations

A general lack of understanding in our society about the impact of homicide is often compounded by poor communication. Although homicide is often in the news and in popular entertainment, people are often unsure of how to talk about it when it hits close to home. You may find some people withdraw or avoid you, while others ask inappropriate questions. One mother of a homicide victim found, when speaking of her daughter's violent death that those whom she was addressing reacted with immediate withdrawal. What most people didn't realize is that their reactions can cause additional distress to the survivors.

Some people have specific traditions in their culture around grieving or loss, and if these traditions feel right to you they may provide some outline of how to begin grieving. Many people don't have any cultural traditions to guide them, and are left on their own to try to figure out how much time to grieve is normal or acceptable. You may be given a 3 day bereavement leave at work, and after only days or weeks some people in your life may expect you to be "back to normal" or "over it". Your grieving process should be whatever is right for you, there is no one right way to grieve.

Another challenge that many people find is that members of the community may question the actions of the victim, or directly blame the victim for their own death. People may blame the victim's actions, lifestyle, or choices. People are trying to make sense out of the unthinkable. Homicide is something that is supposed to happen to someone else, somewhere else. When it hits so close to home, it can make people feel vulnerable, and make the world around them feel unsafe. Blaming the victim is one way to feel like they are in control again. For some people it's easier to think that the victim must be at fault for his or her own death. If not, it could happen to anyone. But in reality, no one deserves to be murdered.

Additional Complications

With a death that is anticipated, such as from an illness, there is time to prepare. With an unanticipated death, such as homicide, there is no time to prepare for the loss. The death is sudden and unexpected, which leaves no time for preparing oneself for the harsh reality. There is no time to say goodbye, the news is typically delivered by a stranger, and often information about your loved one or what happened is scarce. It can seem like chaos with either too much or not enough information about what happened. There may be concerns about others that are involved. It may just seem like a bad dream or that it could not possibly be true that your loved one has been murdered. All of the emotions you may be feeling are reactions that are typically seen by those who have lost a loved one to a violent death.

The loss of a loved one through a violent death can be made worse by previous difficult situations in a person's life. You may have had past losses or trauma. There are numerous past issues in a person's life that can multiply the emotions felt after a violent loss. There may be more than just bereavement for your loved one; it may feel as if everything from your past has turned your world upside down. The term for this is complicated grief. As time goes on, being aware of the past losses, recognizing how they impact your life, both now and in the past, and getting support will be helpful in your grief journey.

As you work with your grief many people find that taking care of the day to day needs is a struggle. There may be funeral arrangements to be made; there may be an investigation and the beginning of the court process, belongings to be taken care of, family members to notify, etc. The details may seem overwhelming. While you may be wondering how you will get through another day, the world around you keeps on going. Others are going to work, school, grocery shopping and taking care of all of the details of living life. This may be difficult as you may feel as if your life has come to a standstill. Using and communicating with your support network will be especially important during this time. Allowing others to do for you may be the only way they know how to show their support and caring.

Conclusion

The grieving process after the death of a loved one by murder is as personal as the memories of that loved one. Everyone moves through the process differently and at their own pace. There is no right or wrong way to heal and find a new 'normal' in your life.

You may hear people speak of 'stages of grief'. There are no specific steps you go through, or in any particular order. There are common experiences that many survivors share. This chapter has tried to lay out for you common feelings, thoughts and stories that other survivors have shared. You may find comfort knowing that what you are feeling or dealing with has happened to someone else.

There are no magic words or magic formula to help you heal. Healing comes from the passage of time and the ability to talk about what has happened. Find someone, or others,

Victim Support Services

who share your kind of loss. Talking to them, telling your story, sharing memories of your loved one will help you move from victim to survivor.

Chapter 2

Coping

It is not uncommon to feel hopeless after a loved one has been murdered. It is difficult to believe that anyone can survive such a debilitating loss, let alone find meaning in living. Yet, survivors somehow find ways to continue. Identifying ways to carry on, to find meaning in living, and sustain the memory of your loved one helps towards gradually lessening the pain and hopelessness over time.

Do not be surprised at the intensity of your feelings once the shock and numbness subsides. You are now trying to cope with an incredibly stressful event that was out of your control. It can be difficult at first, but reestablishing some sort of control over your life can go a long way towards rebuilding.

Victim Support Services

Basics of coping for survivors

Taking care of one's self is not something that comes natural to everyone. It is challenging for most people every day. After a loved one has been murdered it can be even more difficult. However, the best remedy for getting through a difficult time is prescribing the basics of **self-care**:

- Try to get enough rest, eat a balanced diet, and find ways to relax so that you can face what lies ahead
- Do your best to maintain a normal routine even when it is difficult. Putting more structure into a daily routine will help one to feel more in control
- Exercise, relaxation, and distraction are some ways that people use to restore themselves and gain energy
- It may be helpful to keep lists, write notes, or keep a schedule
- Drink plenty of water
- If you consume alcohol, drink it in moderation. Alcohol should not be used as a way of masking the pain
- Remember other difficult times and how you have survived them, draw upon that inner strength
- Take it one moment, one hour at a time, and one day at a time
- Ask for help and share your needs with others

Remember that everyone is different. There is not one way to process and handle your grief. What works for you may not work for others. Give yourself breaks, allow for grace, and remember that it takes time. The *Self Care Strategies* table outlines some different ideas of how to practice self-care.

Self-Care Strategies

Physical Caring	Emotional Caring	Spiritual Caring
<ul><li>Regular exercise</li><li>Sleep</li><li>Healthy eating</li><li>Drinking enough water</li><li>Humor and laughter</li><li>Pilates or Yoga</li><li>Relaxation techniques (deep breathing, meditation)</li><li>Massage, bubble baths, spa activities</li><li>Repetitive activities (sewing, quilting, walking, hiking, sports, woodworking, drawing, cooking, games, etc.)</li></ul>	<ul><li>Nurturing healthy relationships</li><li>Connect with people that make you feel good, who can offer support, a shoulder to cry on or a joke to give you a little boost.</li><li>Counseling</li><li>Talking/venting</li><li>Support Groups</li><li>Reflection and Journal Writing</li><li>Art (painting, sculpting, photography)</li><li>Meditating</li><li>Poetry</li><li>Movies, Books, Music</li><li>Volunteering</li><li>Setting boundaries with difficult people and situations</li></ul>	<ul><li>If you participate in religious activities, reaching out to your faith community may provide some comfort</li><li>Time with art, nature, or music</li><li>Meditation</li><li>Prayer</li><li>Solitude</li><li>Reading</li><li>Visiting the grave or columbarium</li></ul>

Victim Support Services

Handling difficult feelings

It is difficult to begin identifying ways to handle the fury of feelings that progress after the loss of your loved one. Feelings of sadness, fear, guilt, and/or anger can be very distressing and may interfere with your ability to function in your daily life.

It may help to figure out what the feelings are and come up with ways to cope that may lessen the intensity of those feelings. For example, journaling or talking about your experiences and feelings might help bring clarity about what is most troubling. Sometimes taking time to journal or place words on the feelings that you are experiencing can release its power over us, and help us find strategies towards coping.

Assessing how reasonable your feelings are can be difficult. Sometimes our emotions are based on inaccurate or unhelpful beliefs. Try to place your feelings into perspective by challenging their validity. Think about how realistic it is that you could have changed the events that led up to the murder. Naming, evaluating, and accepting our feelings may allow us to find ways to process through our grief. Counselors and therapists can often help guide survivors through these intense feelings, and can help to establish a plan to move forward.

Try your best to calm down when feelings get especially strong, or when you experience panic attacks. Relaxation exercises like slow breathing, and meditation may help. Sometimes removing yourself from upsetting situations, exercising, listening to music, and distracting yourself with something that takes your attention away from the issue at hand can help. You may consider consulting with your medical provider if these events seem to be interfering with your ability to maintain a daily routine for an extended period of time. It may also be comforting to ask close friends for support and help during these times.

Memories

One of the hardest parts of a violent death is when our mind fixates on the person who died and how they died. Violent death unlike natural death is sudden and traumatic. Thoughts about how your loved one died can be very upsetting. Even remembering pleasant memories of a person who has died may be bittersweet, this is a normal part of grieving. Sometimes replacing those difficult memories with positive memories of your loved one can help restore balance.

Some survivors find it helpful to commemorate or memorialize the positive memories of their loved one. Building a memorial garden, planting a tree, or creating a collage are all meaningful ways of helping us remember the pleasant memories of those whom we've lost. Some survivors have started memorial foundations in memory of their loved one.

Counseling

Many survivors have found counseling to be helpful after the loss of a loved one. Some counselors specialize in grief and trauma. A counselor may be able to give you tools for coping, and help you process your loss. Finding a counselor who is a good match for you is a personal decision. Most counselors are happy to talk to you on the phone about their experience and what you hope to accomplish with counseling before setting up your first session. Remember that you are the consumer and it is reasonable to ask about the services you will be receiving. There is no "right time" to see a counselor; it has to happen on whatever timeline is right for you.

Coping for the Long-term

A lot of survivors wonder what it will be like 10 – 15 years down the road. Will you still have sleepless nights or panic attacks? Everyone's journey is a little bit different, every timeline is different, and every loss is unique. However, most people gradually feel better and eventually find ways to continue on living with their loss. In the beginning this may be hard to imagine, but with both time and strong support you may find yourself being able to regain some normalcy back into your life.

Chapter 3

After the Murder

Death Notification

One of the most significant moments after a loved one has been murdered, is the moment you received the death notification. For many, the journey begins that very moment you received the knock on the door; the ring of the bell or cell phone, shortly followed by the words, "This is the police. I'm sorry to inform you that your daughter (son, husband, wife, brother, sister, etc.) has been murdered." In that brief moment, your life has forever changed. You have been traumatically rushed into a new horrific reality from which there is little to no reprieve, a life without your loved one. No matter how sensitive that information is delivered, the horrific news is beyond imaginable.

For many survivors, the moment of notification holds a

vivid memory in their journey, often filled with pain and anger. How you were notified can have lasting impacts on your grief process. Proper death notification should be made in person in a sensitive and humane manner by law enforcement and a trained advocate, spiritual counselor, or support person. An inappropriate and insensitive notification can prolong the grieving process and even delay recovery from the crime. You may not remember every word that was shared during the notification, but the essence of the words and the manner in which they were delivered stay with survivors forever.

Some survivors receive no notification, either because they were present at the time of the murder, or discovered their loved one's body. In some cases family members learn of their loved one's death by watching the news, through social media, or receiving a call from the hospital, neighbor or friend. The reality is that information travels much faster than traditional procedures. Verifications of identity in some cases take time, where speculation from media takes only a few seconds.

The truth is that the moment of notification is inherently traumatic, no matter how sensitive the news is delivered; it simply cannot lessen the impact of learning that your loved one has been murdered. The news often lands on top of you like a 15 ton truck loaded with bricks. It is important to have a support person, someone you can trust to help you notify others in your family, and assist you in making arrangements and plans moving forward.

Funeral Arrangements and Viewing

After receiving notification that your loved one has been murdered, planning funeral arrangements and handling communications with the medical examiner or coroner's office may seem like an impossible task. You may find that identifying someone whom you trust to assist you with these tasks to be helpful.

After a murder, the medical examiner or coroner's office takes responsibility to determine cause and manner of death. They make this determination during an autopsy. Processing what happened to your loved one, and the manner in which they died can be unbearable. Some survivors feel like they need to know every detail outlined in the autopsy report while others may want as little information as possible. Knowing the details about the cause and manner of death is a very personal decision, and different for each individual. If you do wish to know more specifics about the cause and manner of your loved one's death, you may request a copy of the autopsy report, normally for a fee. It is important to note that the details outlined in an autopsy report may be graphic and extremely difficult to comprehend. If you still choose to receive a copy of this report, you may find it helpful to have someone with you when you first process that information.

While your loved one's body is at the morgue, you may feel powerless over what may happen to your loved one. You may feel an overwhelming need to be with them, to hold them, and to view them. Whether or not you would like to view your loved one's body is an extremely personal decision that each person must make for themselves. It can be helpful to talk over this decision with supportive people in your life, as well as your advocate. Many medical examiners and coroners offices discourage viewing of your loved one's body. If positive identity is of concern, they will often seek every other alternative means before having a survivor make the positive identification. If you wish to view your loved one, you most often need to coordinate this through the medical examiner's office or funeral home. If you do decide to view, it is important to have a trusted support person or advocate with you. This process is very emotional, and you may want to find someone that can drive you to a safe place after.

When making funeral arrangements it is important to know your options. Mortuary services are a business, and different companies have different prices. Be sure to bring a trusted friend or support person with you that can help advocate on your behalf. Also, there may be compensation funds available in your state to assist you with these costs. Speak with an advocate in your community to identify what resources might be available to you.

Crime Victim Compensation

No one is ready for the sudden traumatic loss of their loved one. Many survivors worry about the financial costs associated with providing their loved one with a funeral or memorial. State Crime Victim Compensation programs reimburse victims for crime related expenses including medical costs, mental health counseling, funeral/burial costs, and lost wages. Although each state compensation program is administered independently, most programs have similar eligibility requirements and offer comparable benefits.

Compensation is paid when other financial resources, such as private insurance and offender restitution, do not cover the expenses. Some expenses not covered by most compensation programs include theft, damage, and property loss.

Community-based advocacy programs can assist victims with filling out forms and submitting them to their state program. There are limits on how long you have to apply for and use this assistance, as well as specific eligibility requirements, so make sure you check the rules for the program in your state.

The funding for the Crime Victim Compensation program comes from criminal fines, forfeited bail bonds, penalties, and special assessments collected from offenders, not from taxpayers.

Probate and other Benefits

When a person dies, his or her estate must go through probate, which is a process overseen by a probate court. If the decedent leaves a will directing how his or her property should be distributed after death, the probate court must determine if it should be admitted to probate. If the person who has died does not leave a will the court appoints a personal representative or a person who manages the financial affairs of another person who is unable to do so in order to distribute the person's property according to the laws of who should acquire the property. In general, the probate process involves collecting the decedent's possessions, settling obligations, paying necessary taxes, and distributing property to recipients.

In many states individuals may file probate without

the assistance of an attorney, or may be able to avoid the process all together if the total assets of the decedent are limited. Every state outlines their probate codes distinctly so it is important to review the laws that apply in your state. It may also be beneficial to seek legal advice from an attorney to begin this process.

In addition to probate, the decedent's family may have additional death benefits available through the social security, employee pension funds, and other life insurance policies. Locating important documents within the deceased belongings might assist determining which benefits might apply.

Working with the Media

Homicides are usually reported by the news media. Reporters may or may not contact you about the case. You are under no obligation to speak to reporters if you don't want to. If you choose not to talk to reporters, be aware that many will still write stories based on the police report, court documents, or court hearings. You may decide that you want to work with a reporter to tell your loved one's story. It is your right to control if this happens and when. Don't be afraid to say, "I'm not ready to talk now, but when I am I'll call." When the investigation is ongoing, it is important to be careful to share anything with the media that could compromise the case.

To minimize the impact of trespass by unscrupulous reporters, you may exercise the following options:

    1. Refuse to grant an interview

2. Refrain from posting details of the case to social media where reporters may find and repeat that information
3. Appoint a person of your choice to represent your position to the media
4. Submit a written statement rather than undergo an interview
5. Schedule interviews at your convenience
6. Request a specific reporter meet with you
7. Choose who is or is not going to be present during an interview
8. Be informed in advance of the scope of the interview and veto or accept any inquiries at your discretion
9. Review and edit any quotations credited to you or your spokesperson
10. Demand a retraction in response to inaccuracies that have been published
11. Present your side of the story
12. Ask that offensive photographs or visuals be eliminated from a publication
13. Control the size of the news conference
14. Refuse media contact during criminal proceedings, particularly those that might jeopardize your case
15. Refuse to share your grief in public
16. Ask law enforcement to advise you what not to share about the case

Even if you exercise these options, remember you cannot control what the reporters ultimately say or do. When reading, watching, or listening to the news stories, remember that while most reporters try to be as accurate as possible, they do sometimes make mistakes, or don't have the whole story. Take things you see in the media with a grain of salt, especially reader comments.

NOTES:

Chapter 4

The Criminal Justice System

The criminal justice system, as a whole, can be quite daunting and difficult to understand due to its size and complexity. From the moment a crime happens, victims may have to engage with the criminal justice system in some form or another. From reporting or learning about the crime, through the investigation phase, and a potential criminal trial. You probably have some questions about how the criminal justice system works. None of your questions are foolish. The criminal justice system can be confusing, frightening and, at times, absolutely frustrating.

Even though many components of the criminal justice system are similar, the location of the crime determines what steps will occur next. Terminology also differs from state to

Victim Support Services

state. Some places call the person responsible for holding the offender accountable a prosecutor. Others refer to this person as a District Attorney or United States Attorney. The important thing to remember is that their responsibility is to hold the offender accountable for their actions.

It is important to remember that those who administer our laws, i.e., police officers, prosecutors, judges, etc., hear and see the worst of society every day. As a necessity, many build self-protective barriers which occasionally come across to victims as insensitive. Police officers, prosecutors and judges care a great deal and want to see the offender held accountable for the harm they caused. If you feel communication is an issue, or that you have been treated unfairly, contact your local victim advocate.

For most people this will be their first encounter with the criminal justice system. It is not like television. The police generally cannot provide around-the-clock protection for you or your family. The offender often is not arrested immediately, the prosecuting attorney does not stumble upon a surprise witness at the last moment—causing the defendant to cry "I'm guilty!" and the system does not work as quickly as movies and television programs would have us believe. Television shows such as CSI also skew opinions about what forensic testing can actually be conducted. In many cases, forensic evidence does not exist.

Investigation

Law enforcement officers are solely responsible for investigating the case to identify who perpetrated this horrific crime against your loved one. In some cases, law enforcement officers may need your assistance in getting information about your loved one. Sometimes the family may need to be ruled out as potential suspects. While this can be very offensive and painful, inter-family violence is not uncommon, and often the perpetrator is someone the victim knew.

During the initial stages of the investigation, law enforcement may not be able to give you very much information about the case and who perpetrated the crime. This can be very frustrating and it may seem to you as if nothing is being done with your case. At times you may find that the media has more information about your case than you do; this is because the media has access to information through a variety of sources other than law enforcement. However, to secure the integrity of the investigation some details of the investigation may need to be kept confidential. Working with a victim advocate might assist you in obtaining more information about the status of the investigation, and may provide you access to some of the information you are looking for. However, sometimes despite the best efforts of advocates, some information may just not be available.

In many cases, arrests and formal charges are not made right away. Unlike "Law & Order" and "CSI", murder investigations take time. In order to build a solid case, a large amount of evidence needs to be collected and analyzed. It is often better for investigators to take their time and do things right the first time, rather than risking a mistrial, appeal, or formal dropping of charges for a mistake.

As a survivor, it may be physically, emotionally, and mentally draining to wait out this process. You may find yourself losing hope if you see time pass without any arrest. It is important to know that for some cases, it just takes time. An arrest may be made down the line. Someone, somewhere, knows something. Building a strong support system to help aid you during this time may help.

Communication and Logistics

During the initial stages of the investigation it is important to identify a point of contact for you and your family with the law enforcement agency, prosecuting attorney's office, and medical examiner. It may be helpful to purchase a spiral bound notebook to track all the pertinent information to assist you. During the immediate aftermath, you may want to identify someone whom you trust to take notes for you, and act as a second pair of eyes and ears during meetings and while setting up arrangements. Due to trauma and grief reactions you may find it difficult to remember specific details or points discussed, and having a support person may be helpful.

As the investigation proceeds it may make sense to designate one or two family representatives that can act as the main point of contact for the family when new information arises and information needs to be disseminated. With large families it may be difficult for law enforcement and other agencies to contact family members individually.

If information surfaces that law enforcement is unaware of and may be pertinent to your case, call the investigating officer and relay the information you learned. If you're not sure who to talk to, your local advocate can assist you with this.

Cold Cases

Cold case is a term used to describe unresolved cases. This happens when all leads have been exhausted and have resulted in no viable suspects. However, with recent developments with DNA technology, investigators are sometimes able to re-examine past cases and discover new leads. In addition to new DNA evidence, other forms of evidence may arise that reignite a cold case such as new witnesses, confessions, or anonymous tips.

When a case goes "cold" survivors often feel a range of emotions including hopelessness, pain, frustration, and isolation. These emotions are certainly normal and valid given the circumstances. When cases go by with so many unanswered questions as to who perpetrated this crime against your loved one, the grieving process may become more difficult. For many, these unanswered questions may delay progress and healing. It is important to build a strong support system to help assist you with the range of these emotions and additional complications that you may encounter. Working with a counselor or therapist might assist you in identifying positive ways to cope with these unanswered questions. You might also find peer support groups helpful.

The Prosecutor's office

After the investigation is underway, enough evidence has been collected to establish probable cause, and law enforcement has a suspect, the case goes to the prosecuting attorney for charging. The decision to charge a case is solely in the hands of the prosecuting attorney, not the family or the detective. Many prosecutors appreciate feedback from the detective and family. This feedback can come into consideration regarding a charge but does not necessarily affect the outcome of the case due to complications from the legal system. If charges are filed, court documents will read "STATE OF _____ v. defendant" but in some areas you may see "People v. defendant" or "Commonwealth v. defendant". There are legal considerations which factor into the decision of the actual charges filed, i.e., first-degree murder, second-degree murder, or manslaughter. For those that do not have legal experience, this can be confusing and frustrating.

If your state currently has the death penalty, the crime occurred in a time that the death penalty was still a form of punishments and/or the crime is in under federal jurisdiction, this charge can be pursued by prosecutors as well. Just as prosecutors have legal guidelines that need to be followed when deciding the ultimate charge for a case, additional legal guidelines need to be established before pursuing a death penalty case. These additional legal guidelines are referred to as aggravating factors. Depending on the location where the crime occurred, a determination will be made as to what aggravating factors have occurred. To get an inclusive list of aggravating factors, please contact your local law enforcement, prosecutor or advocate.

The complexity of the legal system, and the numerous ways a homicide can be charged can generate feelings of confusion and at times, resentment. The charge the prosecutor decides on is not an indication of the value of the victim's life or that the system favors one victim compared to the next. The charge the prosecutor decides to go forward with is a reflection of the law and the legal elements of the criminal act that need to be proven in court. However, the charge will be based on what the prosecutor can prove, not necessarily what law enforcement or the prosecutor knows or think occurred.

In most states, victims have rights that entitle them to be notified of court hearings and plea deals. Most prosecutor offices prefer to have one representative act as the main point of contact for the family. Be sure the person you select has good communication and listening skills so your concerns are well communicated to the prosecutor and the information provided by the prosecutor is relayed to other family members in a timely fashion. It is not uncommon for families to be divided so one point of contact is not always beneficial. You may want to identify more than one point of contact if this applies to you. At any time, regardless if you are the main contact for the family or not, you can always contact the prosecutor or victim advocate directly.

Courts

There are multiple courts structures within the overall judicial system. These include Superior, Federal, Tribal and Juvenile. Courts hear cases depending on jurisdiction which is determined by where the crime was committed. Another component regarding which court your case will be processed through is specific circumstances of the homicide. Each of these specific court systems focus on the law of the geographical area where the crime occurred. Laws vary from state to state, and are unique to specific territories and age of the offender as well. While there are different court systems there is a certain overlap between all.

Superior Court

Most homicide cases are heard by the general jurisdiction of the state's superior court. Most states have two types of superior courts. First is trial court, better known as Superior Court. Second is referred to as appellate courts, made up of the Court of Appeals. Since perpetrators maintain the presumption of innocence, they assume the legal rights of the accused including the right to a fair trial. These rights are monitored by the state's judicial officer in superior court.

Due to the serious nature of homicide cases, superior courts obtain the legal authority either by the felony classification outlined through a probable cause statement (document listing the charges) and signed by a presiding judge, or is determined through indictment (document listing the charges) found by a grand jury. Superior court has general jurisdiction over other lesser courts (district or municipal) and is considered a higher court.

Superior court judges are elected by voters of the region and are considered nonpartisan officials. Each court consists of a judicial officer (better known as a judge or commissioner), a court clerk, court reporter, and bailiff. The court clerk helps the judge manage cases, keep court records, deal with financial matters, and give other administrative support to the judge and the court as a whole. The court reporter writes down word for word, what is said during the proceedings. That information is collected by a stenographic machine, shorthand, or a recording device. Finally, there is a court bailiff who is in charge of the security of the court including evidence admitted and the jury.

The clerk's office acts as the official record keeper of superior court. The clerk's office can help if you would like to receive copies of court records, confirm court dates, and can provide you with information about what documents have been filed with the court.

Federal Court

Federal court focuses on violations to the United States constitution and federal law. There are times that a case may start out in superior court and then be designated to federal court. Federal courts work in a different manner than superior courts. In superior court, all proceedings are open to the public. You can also obtain reports of what occurred in court. Under the federal system, obtaining information of this kind is limited. Numerous hearings are also closed to the public. That means that even family cannot attend the hearings. It is not uncommon for families to become frustrated with the lack of information Federal prosecutors are allowed to tell you. If this is a death penalty eligible case, the family will never know how or why the court chooses to pursue the death penalty or not. One unique feature of federal court is that you can register to be notified of all proceedings automatically. Victim Notification System (VNS) will give you case information and notification when a court date has been continued and rescheduled. Some superior courts have this capability but it is not widespread like the federal system.

Tribal Court

Tribal courts were created to hold offenders accountable in geographic areas designated as Native American land. The creation of such courts was to continue the religious and cultural traditions of Native Americans. Many tribal courts focus on restorative justice. Restoring the balance between those wronged and the offender is a primary focus. Superior and federal courts are punitive in nature and focus primarily on punishing the offender.

For a case to proceed in tribal court, the offender, victim or both need to be of Native American heritage. For crimes that occur on reservations and the victim and or offender do not have such a status, federal court will have jurisdiction. Even if the victim, offender or both are of Native American heritage, homicide cases are referred to the federal system. Tribal courts are very complex systems. To find out more about tribal courts, it is important to contact a local advocate that is knowledgeable within the particular tribal court you are interested in.

Juvenile Court

If the offender is under eighteen years of age, juvenile court will have jurisdiction to hear the case. The primary focus of juvenile court, or in some areas children's court, is rehabilitation. For homicide cases, even though the child may initially be under the jurisdiction of juvenile court, they can be tried as an adult. Some courts will have a decline hearing to determine which court will have jurisdiction. In other states, prosecutors may file a motion and the case is automatically transferred to superior court. Many youth offenders will have a probation counselor assigned from the beginning of the case to act as a liaison between the court and the child. To find out more about juvenile court it is important to contact your local advocate.

Advocates

Victim advocates provide a variety of support services for victims of crime. Advocates based in prosecutor offices or law enforcement agencies provide information and support as you move through those particular criminal justice systems. They are typically not available evenings and weekends and the support they provide ends when their involvement in your case ends. You also may wish to obtain some additional support from a community victim advocate. Supplementary assistance from an agency outside of the criminal justice system can prove to be beneficial.

Community based advocates have generally dealt with the criminal justice system extensively, thus they can provide valuable information and support. Community based advocacy agencies normally have 24-hour crisis lines so an advocate is available to speak with evenings and weekends. These advocates can also help connect you with resources that may not be directly related to the crime. They can assist you with filling out crime victim compensation forms, educate you about the criminal justice system, accompany you to court proceedings to provide emotional support, advocate for your rights in court and assist you in writing a victim impact statement. Services provided by community based advocates are typically free of charge.

Another important distinction between system based and community based advocates is that the services the community based advocates provide do not end when the criminal justice process is over. Community based advocates are there to assist you and provide support and resources as long as you want. Community based advocates are not attorneys and do not give legal advice. Information about how to locate a community advocate can be found at the back of this book.

Hearings and Trial

There will be a number of court hearings for the defendant. Many hearings occur as a matter of the judicial process; others may only happen if a motion is brought before the court. Your advocate may be able to accompany you to any of these hearings, or attend in your absence if you like. Typical hearings are explained in the following sections.

Charging/Probable Cause

Commonly there will be a preliminary hearing, outlining criminal information to establish probable cause. This hearing is typically the offender's first appearance in court. Probable cause refers to facts or evidence that would lead a reasonable person to believe the defendant committed the crime. If probable cause is not established, the case cannot proceed. In some areas, the defendant may have to be present in front of a grand jury. This will be a hearing based on the evidence the prosecution has to establish probable cause. The grand jury will decide if there is enough evidence to go forward with the case or not. In other areas instead of having a grand jury decide if there is enough evidence to go forward with a case, the decision is up to the presiding judge.

Arraignment

After probable cause has been established, an arraignment will occur. An arraignment is when the defendant formally enters into a plea in court. The plea can be guilty to the charge or not guilty. Most courts will not accept a guilty plea at arraignment. This is because the court wants to know that the defendant entered the plea knowingly and intelligently. Judges prefer that a defendant be advised of all possible outcomes of entering a plea and that the defendant has an opportunity to speak with an attorney before any plea consideration.

The arraignment is the start of the time clock for the case. Defendants have the right to a quick and speedy trial so once the defendant has formally entered into a plea in court, the clock starts ticking. You are also likely to get future court dates at the arraignment hearing as well. These dates typically include pretrial hearings and a trial date. Once an original trial date is set, it will likely be changed or continued many times before the trial actually begins.

Pre-trial Hearings

The next step in the court process is pretrial hearings. These hearings may be referred to as omnibus, pretrial conferences or status hearings. The purpose of these hearings is to keep the court aware of the progress of the case. Due to speedy trial laws, it is important to have the defendant present in court in case these rights need to be waived. Even though the law states that a defendant in custody has the right to trial within sixty days (ninety if the defendant is out of custody) this seldom occurs. This can be an especially frustrating part of the judicial process. It takes about a year or longer for a many homicide cases to go to trial. Keep in mind this is the average time the court takes to get a case ready for trial. Some cases take years before the defendant stands trial.

Other hearings may include motions regarding the defendant's statements made to law enforcement, what physical evidence can be admitted into trial and limit areas of conversation from witnesses during testimony. The types of motions brought before the court vary from case to case. If a defendant did not say anything to law enforcement, a motion regarding the defendant's statements is not relevant. If evidence was collected properly, motions to suppress evidence may not occur. It is important to stay in contact with your advocate to ensure you are informed of any and all motions for your specific case.

Negotiations and Plea Agreement

It is not uncommon for many cases to conclude by plea negotiations and agreements made by the prosecutor and the defense counsel. Typically, if a plea negotiation is considered, the prosecutor and prosecutor's advocate will inform the family before a deal is made. This can include a formal meeting so the prosecutor can consider family input. Even though family cannot dictate the prosecutor to offer a plea deal or go to trial, wishes of the family may be taken into consideration. Often, families do not want to go through the heartache of a trial so a plea deal is in their best interest. Families may not want to bear the anxiety of appeals for years and if a plea deal is accepted, it's a definitive action instead of risking the possibility of having a case retried because of the outcome of an appeal. Complications may arise with a case that provokes the prosecutor to offer a plea deal instead of watching the offender walk free. Homicide cases are complex, so there are many reasons why a prosecutor may or may not want to go to trial.

When a defendant decides to accept a plea deal, a plea hearing date will be set. This is the time that the defendant formally enters a guilty plea in front of the judge. In most cases, sentencing is scheduled for a future date. This gives family and friends ample time to prepare victim impact statements to present to the court. In most cases the defendant will enter a guilty plea. There are certain circumstances that the defendant will enter into a plea of no contest or an Alford plea.

No contest is a plea that the defendant does not accept or deny any responsibility but will accept the appropriate punishment for a crime. Not all courts will allow a no contest plea. Even though the defendant is not formally admitting guilt, the consequences of entering such a plea remain the same as pleading guilty. If the defendant pleads no contest they give up their right to appeal. The main difference is that if a civil lawsuit is to follow after the criminal proceedings are over, this plea cannot be used against them in any other action taken.

Alford pleas are another alternative plea to guilty. An Alford plea is similar to a plea of no contest. Both pleas state that the defendant is not accepting guilt for the crime but will accept the appropriate punishment. Most times when an offender enters an Alford plea they claim they cannot remember what occurred, so therefore cannot admit guilt, but is aware that the evidence presented against them will likely result in a conviction at trial. Just as "normal" guilty pleas end the potential of appeals, so does an Alford plea.

Trial

When the trial finally begins, jury selection, also referred to as voir dire, is the initial step. In very rare cases a defendant may waive his/her right to a jury trial. If this occurs the defendant will participate in a bench trial and then the judge will be the one who decides the case.

In most states, trials are open proceedings unless you are going to be called as a witness. Sometimes a family member will be asked to testify at trial as a way to introduce their loved one. Typically after this testimony is complete, they are allowed to remain the courtroom and listen to the rest of the trial if desired. Once witnesses testify, the judge will either dismiss or retain them. Typically those retained for possible future testimony are those involved in law enforcement and have additional information that may need to be addressed at a later time. Retained witnesses cannot sit in on court proceedings until they are released from duty.

It is important to remember to not discuss the case in or around the courtroom at any time. More often than not, jurors are allowed to leave the courtroom for lunch and to go home for the afternoon. You do not want to accidentally encounter a juror and have them overhear conversations about your loved one. This could potentially result in a mistrial. It is best to not discuss what occurs in trial until you are at a safe and private place to do so.

The natural progression of the trial is for the prosecution to present opening statements and then the defense to present theirs. Opening statements are like a story that tells the jury about the case and what they should expect to hear and see regarding testimony. After opening statements conclude, the prosecution will then present their case. It may take days or weeks for the prosecution to present their case. This is due to the fact that the burden to prove the defendant is guilty beyond a reasonable doubt is given solely to the prosecution, not the defense. After the prosecutor rests, the defense has the opportunity to present their case.

It is not uncommon between the time the prosecutor rests their case, and defense begins theirs, that a motion for directed verdict be asked for by the defense. A directed verdict motion occurs when the defense does not feel the prosecution has enough evidence that a jury will be able to convict the defendant on the charges. Usually the defense will ask for the entire case to be dismissed. Other times, it may be only certain components of the case that are requested to be dismissed. The judge has to rule in regard to evidence most favorable to the state (prosecutor) so a directed verdict seldom occurs. More often than not, the jury decides the outcome of the case.

After the defense has presented their case, which may or may not include the defendant's testimony, and is typically quite a bit shorter than the prosecutor's presentation of the case, jury instructions will be discussed. Jury instructions are the written instructions the jury receives to interpret the law and actions regarding deliberation and reaching a verdict. These instructions have all the elements, or components, of a crime. This paperwork will be read aloud in court and a copy of them will be taken back to the jury room.

Closing arguments is the last part of presenting the case. This is an opportunity for the prosecutor to reiterate the evidence showing that the defendant is guilty and an opportunity for the defense to say why the jury should not convict. The prosecutor is the first to start closing arguments, defense follows with rebuttals and then the prosecutor speaks again. Once closing arguments are completed, jury deliberation begins. Waiting for the jury to return with a verdict is often the most stressful part of the trial. There is no way to predict how long a jury will take to reach a verdict. It could take hours or days. If you want to be present when the verdict is read, it's best to be within ten to fifteen minutes of the courthouse.

Another important fact is that at any time prior to the jury handing down the verdict, the defendant can enter a plea of guilty. Once a trial starts this is unlikely to occur but in some circumstances this could happen. If the defendant does enter a guilty plea after trial starts, the jury will be instructed as to what occurred, then be dismissed and the trial will be over. The next step will be setting a date for sentencing.

If the defendant is found guilty or pleads guilty, the judge will set a sentencing date. Most states have sentencing guidelines that are mandated by the federal and state government. The judge is bound by these sentencing guidelines. There is a standard range of time to be served that the judge must consult based on a number of factors. Such factors include the defendant's previous criminal history. Each case is different so it's important to talk to the prosecutor about the sentencing range for your case.

Conduct in Court

Losing a loved on to homicide is the ultimate form of victimization. Having to go to court and see and hear the defendant can be almost too much to bear. It is common for the defendant's families and friends to be present in court as well. It is understandable that emotions will be at an all-time high but it is important to remember that you cannot react outwardly, even though it may be justified. It is important for you to have a tremendous amount of emotional support from your loved ones and victim advocates throughout this emotional ordeal.

The judge will set strict limitations on your emotional behavior in the courtroom. Emotional outburst or other disruptive conduct could be seen as unfairly influencing the jury. You cannot wear clothing that has a picture of your loved one during the trial. You may be directed to sit in a certain area of the courtroom. You cannot talk to the defendant, get close to the defendant or act in an intimidating manner either. If this occurs, you will be asked to leave the courtroom and possibly be ordered by the judge not to return. The reason for these limitations is to avoid the possibility of a mistrial.

It is completely natural to get emotional at times during trial. Tears may be unavoidable, and difficult to suppress. Please keep in mind that if you do get emotional, which is to be expected, you do not want to distract the jury as this could cause complications if the case is appealed. It is completely appropriate to get up and leave during any part of the trial. Seeing gruesome physical evidence and hearing the medical examiner's report of how your loved one died can be extremely painful. There may also be graphic photos shown during the trial. If you are concerned about the photos that might be shown, please talk to your victim advocate. If you would like to see the photos before the trial, often an advocate can sit down with you and show you the photos before the trial starts. If you don't want to see them, let your advocate or the prosecutor know to tell you when they will be shown so you can leave the courtroom. Many times family choose to step out of the courtroom during particularly graphic testimony, like when the medical examiner testifies.

It is possible that your loved one's character will be

defamed by the defense counsel. They are trying to deflect attention away from the defendant. Hearing terrible things said about your loved one is difficult to bear. Victim blaming is common in our society and this is reflected in the court system as well. Just remember that no one deserves to be murdered, no matter what the circumstances were.

It is important to know that sitting through a criminal trial is emotionally and physically exhausting. Remember to be kind and show grace to yourself during this process. Trials open many wounds. You may hear testimony about the homicide that you were not aware of until then. Just remember if you are struggling, reach out to your support system.

Victim Impact Statement

Victim impact statements allow crime victims, during sentencing or parole hearings, to describe to the court or parole board the impact of the crime on their lives. The victim impact statement may include a description of psychological, financial, physical, or emotional harm the victim experienced as a result of the crime. A judge may use information from these statements to help determine an offender's sentence; a parole board may use such information to help decide whether to grant a parole and what conditions to impose in releasing an offender.

A victim impact statement can be presented by verbal testimony, in the form of a letter, or both. You may include a picture of your loved one in the victim impact statement. The victim impact statement is the primary means for you to communicate with the court. It helps the judge get a more complete picture of the defendant's criminal conduct. It also helps the judge in setting restitution claims that are reasonable, accurate, and reflective of the financial loss a family often suffers. Writing a letter can be therapeutic for you as well as informative to the judge. Without it, the judge will only hear the factual side of the case.

The victim impact statement allows you to tell the court who the victim was, how much value the victim had in the lives of his/her family, how your life has been affected since the crime was committed. It helps to create a balanced picture of both offender and victim in determining the most appropriate sentence for the convicted offender.

Many victims have reported that making victim impact statements improved their satisfaction with the criminal justice process and helped them recover from the crime.

Post Sentencing & Appeals

After sentencing, the person who has committed the homicide may be immediately transferred to the Department (DOC) of Corrections. At that point, the Department of Corrections will have sole custody. The offender will be housed within a prison through the Department of Corrections. There may be an adjustment to the length of time the offender will serve, sometimes called "good time". There are different criteria the Department uses to determine this.

Many Departments of Corrections have a victim family notification program. This program can keep you informed of where the offender is located, what the estimated time the offender will serve is, as well as other information. It is important to make sure that the Department of Corrections has updated contact information for you, so that they can keep you informed.

Some people may think that once the sentencing is done there will be closure. We know this is just a part of the grief journey. Some people will find relief, some will just start their grieving and others may feel as if the criminal justice process did not feel like justice at all. The word closure means that there is an end or conclusion. We know there will not be an end to the pain of losing a loved one, although the pain will ease as time goes on.

In cases where the offender was convicted as part of a trial the defendant may, and probably will, file an appeal. Appeals cannot be filed in cases where the defendant pled guilty. In an appeal, the defendant or their attorney is attempting to state that the trial, whether by jury or a judge, contained errors. If the court finds an error that contributed to the trial court's decision, the appeals court will reverse the decision. The prosecuting attorney and defense attorney submit briefs, or papers, to the appeals court and may be granted a court hearing to argue the errors. Once an appeals court
has made its decision, the opportunity for any more appeals is limited. This process takes years and waiting for a decision can be difficult on families.

As part of the defendant's sentence, there may have been restitution ordered. In criminal cases, one of the penalties imposed is requiring return of stolen goods to the victim or payment to the victim for harm caused. In your case, it may be referred to as legal financial obligations. Each state will have a different system to collect restitution; ask the prosecutor or district attorney to explain how restitution is collected in your state.

Criminal Justice Process

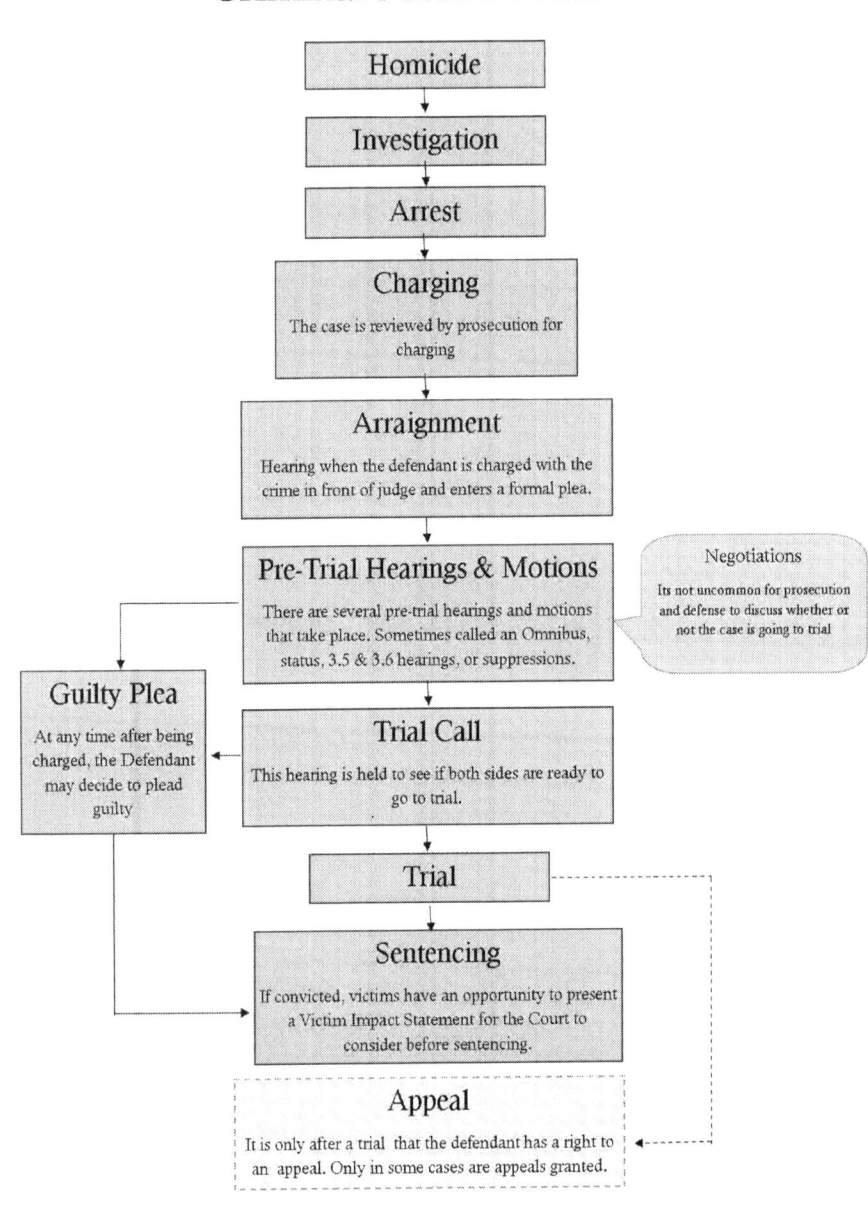

Homicide

Investigation

Arrest

Charging
The case is reviewed by prosecution for charging

Arraignment
Hearing when the defendant is charged with the crime in front of judge and enters a formal plea.

Pre-Trial Hearings & Motions
There are several pre-trial hearings and motions that take place. Sometimes called an Omnibus, status, 3.5 & 3.6 hearings, or suppressions.

Negotiations
Its not uncommon for prosecution and defense to discuss whether or not the case is going to trial

Guilty Plea
At any time after being charged, the Defendant may decide to plead guilty

Trial Call
This hearing is held to see if both sides are ready to go to trial.

Trial

Sentencing
If convicted, victims have an opportunity to present a Victim Impact Statement for the Court to consider before sentencing.

Appeal
It is only after a trial that the defendant has a right to an appeal. Only in some cases are appeals granted.

NOTES:

Chapter 5

Civil Remedies

After a loved one is murdered, it is not uncommon to seek some sort of justice against the person or persons who perpetrated that crime. In some cases, the surviving family members of homicide victims do not find the resolution they wanted through the criminal justice system. When that system fails, some surviving family members have turned to civil justice system to seek financial compensation from the perpetrator or other parties who may hold some civil liability.

Why File a Civil Lawsuit?

Every crime victim has the right to file a civil lawsuit against the perpetrator or other parties whose unreasonable conduct allowed the crime to occur. The civil courts ultimately decide who is liable, and who must pay monetary damages.

Unlike the criminal justice system where the rights of

the case belong to the state, in the civil legal system victims have greater control as they are a listed party in the case. The victim – usually through the representation of a privately attained attorney – controls the essential decisions shaping the case. It is the victim who decides whether to sue, accept a settlement offer, or go to trial.

In addition to greater control, civil actions also provide greater compensation for victims to help cover expenses (medical, property loss, loss of income, etc.) and in some instances cover the emotional damage that they may have suffered.

In some instances, when surviving family members have not had success in the criminal justice system, the civil justice system allows families to hold offenders directly accountable for a crime they committed. Civil lawsuits can sometimes give victims the accountability they seek whether there was a criminal conviction or prosecution in the case at all.

Civil Justice V. Criminal Justice

There are significant differences between the civil and criminal justice system. After a crime happens, the criminal justice process is initiated after a report has been made to law enforcement. If an arrest has been made and charges have been filed, the offender may be prosecuted. The crime is now considered "a crime against the state." The role of victim is primarily as a witness for the prosecution to aid the court in determining guilt or innocence of the accused.

The civil justice system, unlike the criminal justice system, is attempting to determine whether or not the offender or other third-party is civilly liable for the injuries sustained as a result of the crime. In the civil justice system, the "crime" is referred to as a *tort*, or a wrongful act or an infringement of a right leading to civil legal liability. There are numerous types of claims that victims can seek civil actions, some of the claims that homicide survivors sometimes seek are wrongful death or negligence.

Contained within this chapter is a table provided by the National Crime Victim's Bar Association regarding the differences between the civil and criminal justice systems.

Victim Support Services

CRIMINAL CASES In a criminal case…	CIVIL LAWSUITS In a civil lawsuit…
… the goal is to hold the defendant accountable to the State.	… the goal is to hold the defendant accountable to the victim.
… the State prosecutes and controls the case.	… the victim initiates and controls the case.
… the victim is a witness. Although the victim may have rights to participate in the criminal justice process, the victim does not have the right to direct the prosecution of the case or to veto the prosecutor's decisions.	… the victim is a party, and as such, is entitled to all important information relating to the case, and can make important decisions about the case, such as settlement of the claim.
… The State must prove that the defendant is guilty "beyond a reasonable doubt."	… the victim must prove that it is more likely than not that the defendant (or third-party) is liable.
… the defendant is presumed innocent until proven guilty.	… the civil legal system makes no presumption. The victim and defendant appear as equals.
… if a perpetrator is found guilty in a criminal court, the perpetrator is subject to punishment, such as probation or jail, and is held accountable to the State. The victim will not obtain money unless the court orders the defendant to pay restitution for the victim's out-of-pocket expenses. The court cannot order restitution for non-economic damages.	… if the perpetrator is found liable in civil court, the perpetrator owes an obligation to the victim. A civil court can order the perpetrator to pay for non-economic damages, such as pain and suffering, damage to family relationships, and psychological injuries. The civil court can also order punitive damages.
… if the perpetrator is found not guilty, the state cannot initiate a second prosecution.	… the victim can sue the perpetrator in a civil court regardless of whether the perpetrator has been found guilty in criminal prosecution.

National Crime Victim Bar Association. (2013). *Civil Justice for Victims of Crime in Washington.* Washington, D.C. J. Connelly, M. Leeman, S. Royer, & R. Roe.

Hiring an Attorney

It can sometimes be challenging to find the right attorney to take on your case. It sometimes helps to determine what sort of options you have available to you before retaining an attorney. Like most things in life, there are pros and cons. You have to find what is the right fit for you. Take your time, and explore your options. Scheduling initial consultation appointments with three or four different attorneys may help you explore what might be available to you. Many attorneys will schedule a free initial consultation where you can talk about your case and what to expect moving forward.

During the initial consultation it will be important to bring along a list of questions that you might have about the process. Below is a list of potential questions you might want to consider asking:

1. How long will it take to complete the case?
2. How will the lawyer's fees be calculated?
3. What role do I have as a client in making decisions about the case?
4. How will you tell me about plans and problems as the case goes along?
5. Will you answer all of my questions even when they seem unimportant or difficult?
6. What is your experience with cases like this?
7. Do you have the time to work on my case?
8. How long have you practiced law?

It will also help to bring along any case documentation that you have collected since the crime happened including police reports, copies of medical bills, and other documentation that might assist you in explaining your case.

Victim Support Services

The attorney-client relationship is based on the ability for both sides to communicate effectively with each other. It is important that you feel as comfortable as possible disclosing sensitive information to your attorney so that they can represent your interests at their highest ability. A good attorney should be able to explain to you all the aspects of the legal proceedings, and should be responsive to your needs and requests. Make sure to read and fully understand the retainer agreement prior to signing, and do not hesitate to ask questions for clarification if needed.

It is important that you understand all the potential positives and negatives of filing a civil lawsuit. It is a long arduous process that can be both physically and emotionally draining. Civil cases take place in public court, and are open to public disclosure. Though some components of the case may be sealed upon request from your attorney and court ruling, it has the potential of opening up sensitive parts of your personal life throughout the process.

It is important to also learn about the statutes of limitations applicable in your state. In some states you must file a wrongful death suit within three years from the date of death. To learn more, about the civil justice system, contact the National Crime Victim Bar Association's Website www.victimbar.org or 1-844-529-4357.

Chapter 6

Crime Victims' Rights

The Crime Victims' Rights Act, part of the United States Justice for All Act of 2004 enumerates the rights afforded to victims in federal criminal cases. The Act grants victims the following eight rights:

1. The right to be reasonably protected from the accused.

2. The right to reasonable, accurate, and timely notice of any public court proceeding, or any parole proceeding, involving the crime or of any release or escape of the accused.,

3. The right not to be excluded from any such public court proceeding, unless the court, after receiving clear and convincing evidence, determines that testimony by the victim would be materially altered if the victim heard other testimony at that proceeding.

Victim Support Services

4. The right to be reasonably heard at any public proceeding in the district court involving release, plea, sentencing, or any parole proceeding.

5. The reasonable right to confer with the attorney for the Government in the case.

6. The right to full and timely restitution as provided in law.

7. The right to proceedings free from unreasonable delay.

8. The right to be treated with fairness and with respect for the victim's dignity and privacy.

Each state has established their own laws regarding victim's rights. Please check with an advocate to find out what rights you have.

Other Reading

- **"What To do When the Police Leave"** A guide to the first days of traumatic loss. By Bill Jenkins (WBJ Press, Richmond, VA)

- **"No Time for Goodbyes"** Coping with sorrow, anger, and injustice after a tragic death. By Janice Harris Lord (Pathfinder Publishing of California)

- **"When Something Terrible Happens"** Children can learn to cope with grief. By Marge Heegaard (Woodland Press, Minneapolis, MN)

- **"Beyond the Bullet"** Personal stories of gun violence aftermath. By Heidi Yewman

- **"When Bad Things Happen to Good People"** How people can deal with tragedy that enters their lives. By Harold S. Kushner

- **"When Your Child Dies: Tools for Mending Parents' Broken Hearts"** How to navigate the grieving process. By Avril Nagel and Randie Clark

- **"Murder Survivor's Handbook: Real-life Stories, Tips and Resources"** By Connie Saindon and Larry Edwards

- **"The Forgiveness Myth"** How to heal your hurts, move on and be happy again when you can't or won't forgive. By Gary Egeberg and Wayne Raiter

- **"When a Friend Dies"** A book for teens about grieving and the healing process. By Marilyn Gootman Ed.D

Resources

Dougy Center for Grieving Children & Families
503-775-5683 www.dougy.org
Email: help@dougy.org

Parents of Murdered Children and Other Survivors of Homicide (POMC)
888-818-POMC www.pomc.com

National Center for Victims of Crime (NCVC)
800-FYI-CALL www.victimsofcrime.org

National Crime Victim Bar Association (NCVBA)
844-LAW-HELP (529-4357) www.victimbar.org
Email: victimbar@ncvc.org

National Crime Victim Law Institute (NCVLI)
Email: ncvli@lclark.edu or Call 1-888-768-6556 and leave a message. Please say whether it is safe to leave a message when we return your call. It may take 7-10 business days to return your call.

National Organization for Victim Assistance (NOVA)
800-TRY-NOVA www.trynova.org

The National Center for Missing and Exploited Children
www.missingkids.com/home
24-hour call center: 1-800-THE-LOST (1-800-843-5678)

Victim Support Services

Victim Information and Notification Everyday (VINELink)
www.vinelink.com

Victim Support Services
888-288-9221 or 425-252-6081
www.victimsupportservices.org
Email: contactus@victimsupportservices.org

Glossary of Terms

Acquittal: A final judgement by a judge or jury that the prosecution has not proven a criminal defendant's guilt beyond a reasonable doubt. This is a *not guilty* verdict.

Allocution: A formal statement made by the defendant after they have been found guilty, either by plea or jury, prior to being sentenced

Advocacy: Personal support and/or assistance with issues resulting from victimization

Advocate: A person who is trained to support victims of crime. They offer emotional support and information about the criminal justice process and victim rights. They assist with resource navigation, safety planning, and crisis intervention.

Alternate Juror: A juror selected in the same manner as a regular juror who hears all the evidence but does not help decide the case unless called on to replace a regular juror

Appeal: A request made after a trial by a party that has lost on one or more issues that a higher court review the decision to determine if it was correct.

Victim Support Services

Arraignment: A proceeding in which a criminal defendant is brought into court, told of the charges in an indictment or information, and asked to plead guilty or not guilty.

Bail: The deposit, money, property or bond that is put up by or on behalf of an arrested person to get him or her out of jail before or after court proceedings begin. Some charges or cases may be denied bail due to the severity or flight risk of the accused.

Calendar: The list of cases set to be heard in the same court on the same day.

Complaint: A written accusation filed by a prosecutor in court that accuses one or more persons of committing one or more crimes.

Continuance: A delay in Court proceedings

Conviction: A guilty judgement based on the verdict of a jury, a judge or on the plea of guilty or no contest by a criminal defendant.

Count: An allegation in an indictment or information, charging a defendant with a crime. An indictment or information may contain allegations that the defendant committed more than one crime. Each allegation is referred to as a count.

Damages: Money that a defendant pays a plaintiff in a civil case if the plaintiff has won. Damages may be compensatory (for loss or injury) or punitive (to punish and deter future misconduct).

Defendant: A person against whom a criminal case is pending.

Defense Attorney: The attorney representing the defendant; he or she may be a private attorney, a court appointed attorney or from the county public defender's office.

District Attorney: See prosecutor. The individual responsible for reviewing the evidence to determine if formal charges may be filed. Once a case has been filed they then prosecute the case through the final disposition.

Discovery: The pretrial procedure in which the defense receives evidence in the possession of the prosecution, including witness statements, police reports, scientific examinations, etc.

Due Process: The constitutional guarantee that a defendant will receive a fair and impartial trial.

Evidence: Information presented, either through testimony, documents, or material objects to prove or disprove any fact relevant to the case.

Expert Witness: A person who has training, education or experience on a particular subject and is formally found to be qualified as an expert by the judge. An expert may give opinions in court matters where their expertise is relevant.

Felony: A serious crime, usually punishable by at least one year in prison.

Hung Jury: Occurs when jurors cannot unanimously agree on a verdict or either guilty or not guilty and leads to a

Victim Support Services

mistrial.

Information: A formal accusation filed in court accusing one or more persons of committing one or more crimes.

Judgement: The official decision of a court finally resolving the case.

Jury: The group of persons selected to hear evidence in a trial and render a verdict on the facts of the case.

Misdemeanor: A crime punishable by imprisonment of one year or less in the county jail, by fine, or both.

Mistrial: An invalid trial, caused by a fundamental error. After a mistrial has been declared, the trial must start again with the selection of a new jury.

Motion: A formal request by either the prosecution or defense for a judge to hear and decide a dispute relating to the case.

Plea: The defendant's response to formal charge(s) in court by either guilty or not guilty.

Plea Bargain: Occurs when the defendant agrees to plead guilty to a lesser offense or only one of the several charged offenses in return for an agreed upon disposition.

Probation: A sentencing option available to the court to impose that the defendant be supervised by the probation department under specific conditions. Conditions could include some jail time, a fine, restitution to the victim, community service, counseling, and additional conduct conditions.

Prosecutor: See also District Attorney. The individual responsible for reviewing the evidence to determine if formal charges may be filed. Once a case has been filed they then prosecute the case through the final disposition.

Record: A written account of the proceedings in a case, including all pleadings, evidence, and exhibits submitted during the case.

Restitution: The payment made to the crime victim by the defendant for the financial losses or personal injuries caused by a crime.

Sentence: The penalty ordered by a judge and the court for the defendant who has been convicted of a crime.

Sentencing Guidelines: The set of rules established that judges use to determine the sentence for the convicted defendant.

Subpoena: A mandatory notice provided to a witness to appear and testify in court.

Verdict: The decision of a jury that determines the guilt or innocence of the defendant.

Voir Dire: The process by which a jury is questioned to determine their qualification or conflict before a trial.

Victim: Anyone who suffers emotional or physical injuries or who dies as a result of a crime.

Witness: A person who has knowledge about a case and is called upon to testify before the court.

Victim Support Services

NOTES:

NOTES:

Made in the USA
San Bernardino, CA
13 October 2016